CAREERS IN
CRISIS MANAGEMENT & HOSTAGE NEGOTIATION

CAREERS IN
CRISIS MANAGEMENT & HOSTAGE NEGOTIATION

LAURA LA BELLA

ROSEN
PUBLISHING®

New York

Published in 2014 by The Rosen Publishing Group, Inc.
29 East 21st Street, New York, NY 10010

Copyright © 2014 by The Rosen Publishing Group, Inc.

First Edition

Library of Congress Cataloging-in-Publication Data

La Bella, Laura.
Careers in crisis management and hostage negotiation/Laura LaBella.
    pages cm—(Extreme law enforcement)
Includes bibliographical references and index.
ISBN 978-1-4777-1709-7 (library binding)
1. Crisis management. 2. Hostage negotiations. I. Title.
HD49.L3 2014
363.34'8023—dc23

                                                              2013010920

Manufactured in the United States of America

CPSIA Compliance Information: Batch #W14YA: For further information, contact Rosen Publishing, New York, New York, at 1-800-237-9932.

CONTENTS

INTRODUCTION

One of the most famous hostage situations in U.S. history was the abduction of Terry Anderson, a journalist living and working in Beirut, Lebanon, in 1985. Anderson was abducted on the streets of Beirut and held captive for six years and nine months by a group of Hezbollah Shiite Muslims. They systematically held hostages in retaliation for Israel's use of American weapons against Muslim targets in Lebanon.

Criminals and political extremists use the threat of violence to hold individuals hostage. During these situations, hostage-takers use the lives of their hostages as bargaining chips to get what they want. Hostage-takers all have different objectives. Some want to negotiate deals with law enforcement. Others want media attention for a cause. Regardless of the hostage-takers' motives, crisis managers and hostage negotiators are on the front lines of the situation. They are in communication with the hostage-takers and are working to resolve the crisis in a peaceful way.

Crisis managers and hostage negotiators are the calming force within a storm. They manage compelling, edge-of-your-seat, dangerous situations that can mean the difference between life and death. These professionals must be ready for any situation and prepared to put themselves on the line for the safety of others. They must be ready to accept the

Law enforcement professionals are highly trained in crisis management and hostage negotiation. Regular training, like the exercise pictured here, provides professionals with the most up-to-date tactics for effective management of crisis and hostage scenarios.

severity of any given situation. These are not easy jobs. They are stressful and demanding, both physically and mentally. They are jobs for the tough and the experienced.

The emergence of crisis management and hostage negotiation positions is one of the most significant developments to occur within the law enforcement and communication fields over the past several decades. These professionals are skilled at handling high-pressure situations. They are prepared and well trained. They have excellent communication skills and can make good decisions under pressure. Crisis managers and hostage negotiators also have a solid understanding of psychological conditions, they have knowledge of or experience in law enforcement or the military, and they can work with or manage a variety of people. With a wide range of career options and specializations—and in an ever more chaotic and uncertain world—the growth potential in these career fields is limitless.

CHAPTER ONE

UNDERSTANDING CRISIS MANAGEMENT AND HOSTAGE NEGOTIATION

Before the 1970s, crisis management and hostage negotiations were not a regular part of training for law enforcement agencies. But two events helped influence and, ultimately, change how the law enforcement community now handles crisis situations and hostage negotiations. These events are the Attica Prison Riot and the Munich Massacre. Both revealed flaws in how law enforcement officials were trained to carry out crisis situations and negotiations. But these incidents also presented opportunities to improve protocols, enhance planning, and develop training techniques that would later help defuse future crises and save lives.

Attica

In 1971, at the Attica Correctional Facility in Attica, New York, a riot broke out when prisoners demanded better living conditions. The maximum-security prison, often described as being escape- and riot-proof, was designed to hold 1,200

After inmates staged a riot on September 11, 1971, guards prepare to enter the Attica Correctional Facility in an attempt to regain control of the prison after four days of negotiations broke down. In the aftermath, forty-three people (thirty-two inmates and

inmates. At the time, however, it was actually housing 2,225 prisoners.

This overcrowding led to poor living conditions for inmates. Prisoners were allowed to shower only once per week, were given one roll of toilet paper per week, and shared cells originally meant to hold only one person. They felt they had been illegally denied certain rights and basic living conditions. As a result, about one thousand prisoners rioted, seizing control of the prison and taking thirty-three members of the prison staff, including correctional officers, hostage.

The riot lasted four days as negotiations were held between law enforcement and the inmates. Authorities agreed to twenty-eight of the prisoners' demands. But they would not agree to amnesty, a formal form of forgiveness given by the government that would prevent inmates from being prosecuted for their roles in the riot and prison takeover.

When negotiations broke down, the New York State governor, Nelson Rockefeller, ordered state police to forcibly take back control of the prison. Using tear gas and excessive force, the state police raided the prison. When the raid was over, forty-three people (thirty-two inmates and eleven guards) were dead. Thirty-nine of these individuals were killed during the police's attempt to retake the prison.

In the aftermath, it was found that authorities were not prepared or trained to handle a prison riot. Nor was there a plan in place to guide law enforcement officials on what to do if a crisis of this magnitude should occur. While the riot may

Eleven members of Israel's Olympic team were held hostage by armed Palestinian terrorists during the 1972 Olympic Games in Munich, Germany. Two West German policemen, dressed as athletes, tried to get close to the area where the hostages were being held. After several failed rescue attempts, the terrorists killed the athletes. Five of the eight terrorists were killed and the remaining three were captured.

have been caused by inmate behavior, its deadly resolution was the cause of poor crisis management by prison leadership and law enforcement officials.

The Munich Massacre

During the 1972 Olympic Games in Munich, Germany, eleven members of the Israeli Olympic team were taken hostage by a terrorist group called Black September. The group was a Palestinian terrorist organization that seized the hostages while demanding the release of 234 Palestinian prisoners held in Israeli jails and 2 German terrorists imprisoned in Germany.

By the end of a lengthy standoff, which included failed rescue attempts, the

RULES OF CRISIS MANAGEMENT

1. **Be prepared.** Having a plan in place for how you will handle a crisis is pivotal for dealing with the situation. Don't leave crisis management for when a crisis actually arises and is underway. It'll be too late and could cause the situation to become much worse. Create a crisis response plan and practice with the members of your team often so that when a crisis does arise, everyone knows his or her role and what to do as events unfold.

2. **Know what the threats are.** Identify the top threats that your organization could face. Is there a communication plan in place should a gunman enter your school or workplace and you need to evacuate staff? Will your city government have the resources to respond efficiently after a hurricane knocks out power? If the security information for your bank is stolen, how best will you respond and notify customers? These questions and scenarios are best reviewed before a situation arises so that you can immediately begin to handle an event.

3. **Don't remain silent.** You can't ignore a brewing crisis or situation. This will only raise more concerns and increase fear. Crisis managers should communicate often with the public and the media to inform them of what is happening or how things are progressing.

4. **Develop a plan for after the crisis is resolved.** Talk about what you're doing now—the positive steps you are taking or have planned for the future. How you handle the situation after it occurs is just as important as how you handled the situation while it was happening.

5. **Don't lie or cover up the situation.** Lying about a crisis, not matter how serious the emergency, will only make the incident worse. As bad as the truth might be, be honest.

hostage-takers killed the eleven athletes. The standoff showed that German authorities were not prepared or trained to deal with acts of terrorism and hostage-taking. They lacked effective equipment to protect themselves and to communicate with one another, which led to repeated instances of miscommunication. It was also revealed that the German armed forces, which were trained for crisis situations, were not allowed to operate inside Germany during peacetime. These highly specialized military officers were unable to provide assistance during the standoff, leaving the situation to unprepared and inexperienced local authorities.

The Attica Riot and the Munich Massacre illustrated the deep failures within law enforcement to put in place techniques to manage a crisis and negotiate the safe return of hostages. The Attica Riot showed how valuable it was to have a crisis management plan in place before an incident occurs. The Munich Massacre forced many European countries to look at their law enforcement teams and review how they are trained and when military-level operations could be used in domestic incidents that occur during peacetime. Many of these European countries went on to establish permanent, professional counterterrorism teams to handle crisis situations.

Dog Day Afternoon

In 1972, prompted by the Attica and Munich tragedies, the New York City Police Department (NYPD) began training its officers in the use of negotiation strategies as a response to a variety of crisis situations. These ranged from hostage/barricade scenarios and kidnappings to personal crises and other critical incidents. One incident in particular proved how valuable and necessary it was for law enforcement officers to be trained in negotiation techniques.

John Wojtowicz robs a Chase Manhattan Bank in Brooklyn and holds eight bank employees hostage for fourteen hours. Using information about Wojtowicz, gathered by law enforcement professionals, police officers begin to negotiate for the release of hostages. The event marks the beginning of a new approach now widely used in hostage negotiation.

John Wojtowicz was looking for a quick cash grab when he attempted to rob a Brooklyn bank. He ended up holding eight bank employees hostage for fourteen hours while police officers surrounded the building. With little experience, the police officers on the scene realized that Wojtowicz didn't want to die. So they began talking to him to understand what was going on. They quickly learned that Wojtowicz had attempted the bank robbery because his partner needed surgery.

Using that information, the officers were able to talk him into thinking that he was going to escape without being arrested. He was apprehended, however, and the hostages were safely rescued. Wojtowicz stood trial and was later sentenced to twenty years in prison. This real-life story inspired the 1975 movie *Dog Day Afternoon*, starring Al Pacino (in which he defiantly taunts the law enforcement officers surrounding the bank with a chant of "Attica! Attica!").

A New Way to Respond

At the time of this incident, NYPD officer Harvey Schlossberg had recently earned a Ph.D. in psychology. He noticed how the officers on the scene were trying to negotiate with Wojtowicz, offering different deals to save the lives of the hostages. Schlossberg became convinced that there were better ways to talk a hostage-taker out of a hostage situation.

Schlossberg began working with the NYPD to develop crisis and hostage negotiation programs to train law enforcement officers in how to effectively deal with these scenarios. Working with Lieutenant Frank Bolz, Schlossberg began formulating guidelines and theories on hostage negotiation. Bolz and Schlossberg trained the first hostage negotiation team for the NYPD.

Bolz and Schlossberg's guidelines have changed very little since they were developed and have been used worldwide as the foundation for negotiation training. Police and law enforcement agencies around the country have duplicated the efforts of the NYPD. These new methods of planning for crisis management and hostage negotiation serve to better protect communities and provide peaceful outcomes to crisis situations.

What Is Crisis Management?

Crisis management is just what it sounds like—the process of managing a crisis or major event that threatens to harm an organization or the general public. These events can range from natural disasters (Superstorm Sandy, Hurricane Katrina), terrorist attacks (September 11, the 2013 Boston Marathon bombings), and school or workplace violence (the Newtown massacre) to political uprisings, defective or tampered products, and technological problems (such as stolen financial information). A situation becomes a crisis when there is an immediate threat to an organization, group, or individual, when the situation is unexpected or a surprise, and when life-or-death decisions need to be made in a very short amount of time.

Crisis management involves more than just dealing with a situation as it's occurring. Professionals in this field are skilled at crafting management plans that anticipate a variety of situations in an effort to lessen the impact of any crisis that may develop in the future. In the aftermath of the 2007 shootings at Virginia Tech, where a gunman killed thirty-two people, college communication offices around the country began to implement emergency management plans.

These plans provided not only college communication offices but also other college departments, such as the emergency response team and campus security, with a specific and concrete plan and clearly outlined duties to ensure efficient handling of an emergency situation should a similar event occur in the future. The plans included training in crisis management and communications and the cooperation and smooth coordination of efforts with local law enforcement authorities.

Having a plan in place before such threats happen can accomplish a number of goals. It can save lives. It can lead to better communication with those at risk. It can lessen the impact of the threat. And it can help lay the groundwork for dealing with the aftereffects of a threat once it has been resolved. A crisis may have significant impacts once it is over, and those problems must be handled in a smart and effective way.

Crisis management covers everything from natural disasters and school and workplace violence to terrorist attacks, like those that occurred on September 11, 2001. Crisis management activities include more than just handling a situation as it occurs. It also involves organizing search, rescue, and recovery operations (as seen here, as rescue workers search Ground Zero in New York for World Trade Center survivors).

What Is a Hostage Negotiator?

A hostage negotiator is a professional in the law enforcement field who is highly skilled in defusing crisis situations that involve hostages. These hostages are held by captors who hope to obtain something in return for the release of their captives.

A hostage situation is a worst-case scenario for law enforcement officers because it places innocent civilians directly in harm's way. Armed intervention becomes very risky, since the hostages themselves can be harmed either by stray bullets or by the hostage-takers. This makes the negotiation the most important aspect of any hostage crisis. A skilled negotiator must find out what the hostage-taker wants (e.g., money, personal safety/asylum, safe passage to another country, the achievement of political goals), whom he or she is, and what it will take to achieve a peaceful outcome. All of this must be achieved while ensuring the safety of the hostages and other bystanders.

There are three phases of a hostage situation: the initial phase, the negotiation phase, and the termination phase. The initial phase is often violent and brief. It lasts as long as it takes for the hostage-takers to make their assault and subdue the hostages. The end of this phase is often marked by the hostage-takers making their demands.

The negotiation phase begins when law enforcement officials arrive on the scene and the demands have been received. This phase can last hours, days, months, or even years. It can also be referred to as "the standoff phase." Physically, nothing about the situation changes greatly. The hostages and the hostage-takers stay in the same place. But this is the most critical phase for law enforcement officers. This phase presents an opportunity for a negotiator to begin to build a relationship with the hostage-takers. Relationships are being developed between everyone involved (hostage-takers, hostages, law enforcement, hostage negotiator, etc.). The negotiator's job comes down to manipulating those relationships in a way that ends the standoff in a peaceful way.

The termination phase is the conclusion to the event. It can be peaceful or violent, but often it is very brief. This phase usually ends in one of three ways: the hostage-takers surrender peacefully and are arrested; police assault the hostage-takers and kill or arrest them; or the hostage-takers' demands are granted and they escape. The fate of the hostages does not necessarily depend on what happens during the termination phase. Even if the hostage-takers give up, they may have killed hostages during the negotiations. Often hostages are killed either accidentally by police or intentionally by their captors during an assault. There have even been cases in which the hostage-takers were granted their demands, but they killed hostages anyway.

CHAPTER TWO

WHAT HAPPENS ON THE SCENE

When a crisis arises or a hostage situation occurs, what happens on the scene can mean the difference between life and death. Crises, by nature, are unplanned, unexpected events that cause alarm and fear, miscommunication, and panic. For crisis managers and hostage negotiators, the initial response to a problem is just the beginning of a process that includes keeping people safe and informed.

On the Scene: Crisis Management

Crisis management doesn't begin when a crisis breaks out. It starts long before with planning and training that can help professionals deal with a situation quickly and efficiently, hopefully preventing it from growing into a large-scale emergency or disaster. Crisis management deals with threats before and after they have occurred, not just during the crisis itself.

A crisis can be anything from a natural disaster that requires the government to step in to help citizens in distress to a technological incident, such as cyberterrorism, in which important governmental or private information becomes vulnerable. It can be workplace violence in which one employee becomes a threat to others or consumer product vulnerability when a product has been found to be dangerous, defective, or tampered with. A faulty product was the cause of a nationwide crisis for Johnson & Johnson when it learned that one of its pain medicines had been the cause of seven deaths.

Tainted Tylenol

In 1982, Johnson & Johnson faced a crisis when seven people in Chicago, Illinois, died after taking extra-strength Tylenol capsules, pain medicine that's easily available in grocery stores and drugstores. It was found that an unknown person had taken bottles of Tylenol off the shelves at a store and tampered with the capsules by adding the lethal chemical cyanide. This person then replaced the tampered capsules in the bottles and returned them to the shelves. People unknowingly purchased the tampered medication.

Johnson & Johnson was not responsible for the tampering of the product. Yet it nevertheless faced a dilemma regarding how it should handle the crisis. It knew that if it did nothing, its reputation as a company that produces safe, effective products would be damaged and business would suffer. Johnson & Johnson decided to be proactive to ensure the safety of its customers. The company assumed responsibility for the incident and immediately recalled all Tylenol capsules

Chicago policeman Albert Frigo sorts through envelopes containing bottles of Tylenol that were turned in to police by concerned citizens. This was part of the effort to remove tainted bottles of the medication from circulation.

from store shelves all over the country, the vast majority of which were very unlikely to be tainted.

But this was only the beginning of the crisis for Johnson & Johnson. It continued to face a serious problem. How would it reintroduce Tylenol to the public and assure its customers that the product was safe to take? The company put a crisis management plan in place. First it changed the Tylenol packaging to include a seal around each bottle's cap, making the product tamper-proof. The company also offered a coupon with a significant discount to motivate people to begin buying the product again. Finally, its sales force made more than 2,200 presentations to the medical community to help restore confidence in Tylenol. Johnson & Johnson's crisis management plan was successful because it took action by putting people's safety first.

The *Exxon Valdez*

But for every crisis that is managed well, there are many more that are not. Exxon, the world's largest international oil and gas company, spilled 11 million gallons of oil into Alaska's Prince William Sound when one of its oil tankers, the *Exxon Valdez*, ran aground. It was the second-worst oil spill in U.S. history up to that point. The oil polluted the waters in Prince William Sound. Hundreds of thousands of animals, from harbor seals and sea otters to bald eagles, orca whales, and numerous fish species, were killed. The spill adversely affected Alaska's fisheries, national parks, beaches, and forests.

The management of the crisis was poor from the beginning. Exxon did not immediately respond to the oil spill, waiting days to send crews to begin cleanup efforts. The company's chairman did not travel to Alaska. Instead, he sent a team of people who were not trained in crisis management or media relations. Exxon repeatedly answered "no comment" to questions from reporters, fueling speculation that the company was hiding something from the public. Finally, the public grew angry at Exxon, which seemed not to be taking the oil spill or its growing impact on the environment very seriously. The company's response made it appear as though Exxon did not care about the people of Alaska, the

Workmen clean up an oil-covered coastline after the *Exxon Valdez*, a tanker carrying 53.1 million gallons of oil, ran aground near Prince William Sound, Alaska. It was the second largest oil spill in the United States, and its effect on the area's environment and economy was catastrophic.

environment, or the damage that the accident caused to the state's tourism and fishing industries.

Tylenol and Exxon are two examples of how important it is to manage a crisis correctly. Even though the tampering crisis was proven not to be Tylenol's fault, Johnson & Johnson still took responsibility for its product and offered solutions to the problem. As a result, the public's faith in Tylenol and in Johnson & Johnson grew. Tylenol continues to be a trusted product for safe pain relief. Conversely, Exxon continues to be viewed negatively by the public for its failure to take responsibility for the oil spill in Prince William Sound.

On the Scene: Hostage Negotiations

Hostage negotiators must arrive on the scene ready to find out what the hostage-taker wants, whom he or she is, and what it will take not only to keep hostages safe but also to ensure that they are released peacefully. Hostage situations can vary greatly depending on what the hostage-taker wants. Their demands can be simple, like money or personal safety. Or they can be complicated, like trying to achieve a political goal or safe passage to another country. Regardless of the wants of the hostage-taker, the negotiator must come ready to listen, sympathize, and offer help to the hostage-takers and the hostages.

When a hostage negotiation occurs, there are two important officials on the scene: the commander and the negotiator. These are the individuals who often are in control of law enforcement activities and in communication with the hostage-takers. It's vital that two different people hold these positions. One of a hostage negotiator's most useful tactics is to cause delays by telling hostage-takers that higher authorities—i.e., the commander—must be consulted before a decision can be made or a concession offered. If the same person holds both roles, that delay tactic isn't an option for the negotiator.

The Commander

The commander is the one person in charge of all law enforcement officials. He or she has authority over the entire scene and all the personnel (police officers, SWAT teams, medical crews, fire and rescue crews) involved in the crisis or hostage situation. Law enforcement will arrive on the scene before a hostage negotiator, and the commander must make sure that the situation is stabilized and secured so that negotiations can begin quickly. The responsibilities of the commander and the law enforcement personnel working under him or her include:

- Isolating the area around the crisis by setting up barriers and keeping people away from harm
- Containing the movement of the hostage-takers to a small area and preventing them from being able to view police activity

Baltimore police officers push media and curious onlookers back as they lock down a section of the city in response to a hostage situation in a nearby office building. A key activity in crisis management is to secure an area to keep people out of harm's way, while isolating the hostage-taker to a small, contained area.

• Evaluating the situation and gathering as much information as possible, which might include whom the hostage-takers are and how many are involved, what they want, how many hostages they have taken, if they are armed with weapons, and what they look like

• Reporting all information that has been gathered, plus information about the event that caused the situation, to the commander and, once on the scene, the hostage negotiator

The Negotiator

The negotiator's priorities at the beginning of a negotiation are to assess the situation and gather as much information as possible. A negotiator must find out about the hostage-takers and why they have taken hostages. This information might include personal data such as name, age, family, job, political affiliations, religious beliefs,

A NEGOTIATOR'S CHECKLIST

When hostage negotiators arrive on the scene, the first thing they do is talk to the law enforcement officers who responded to the emergency call. This is the first set of information that a negotiator has to work with when he or she makes contact with the hostage-takers. Negotiators will often ask the following questions of the first responders in order to gain an understanding of the situation and how it developed:

- What has occurred?
- Who called the police?
- At what time did the occurrence happen?
- Are there any reported injuries—to police officers, to the hostage-takers, to the hostages?
- Has any contact been made with the hostage-takers, and if so, what was the conversation, when did the contact occur, and who initiated it?
- How many hostage-takers are there?
- How many hostages are there?
- Where are the hostage-takers located?

- **Where are the hostages located?**
- **Is there a floor plan for the location where the hostage-takers are holding the hostages?**
- **Are there phones available?**
- **Can the hostage-takers see out of the building?**
- **Are hostage-takers armed with weapons, explosives, chemicals, etc.?**
- **Is there information already gathered about the hostage-takers and the hostages? If police know the names of the hostage-takers, has a check of their criminal record been completed?**

personal problems, emotional or mental problems, or financial problems. Any of this information could give the negotiator insight into the motives driving the situation.

People take hostages for a number of reasons. Hostage-takers can be emotionally or mentally disturbed, or they can be terrorists who are attacking a particular place or making a political statement. It is important for hostage negotiators to communicate directly with the hostage-takers. They must keep an objective point of view and remain calm. They must find out who the hostage-takers are, why they are holding people hostage, what their demands are, who their leader is, and if there is more than one of them.

Sgt. George McGinty, of the Washington State University Police Department, confers with two hostage negotiators from the Lewiston, Idaho, police department as they prepare to approach a church where a gunman is holding hostages. Clear communication by all parties involved in a crisis situation can make a difference in the outcome of a hostage situation.

At the same time that negotiators are gathering information, they are also paying very close attention to the hostage-taker's responses to questions, to the way he or she is acting or moving, and what his or her general attitude is. These pieces of information are helping the negotiator create a psychological profile. A psychological profile is a tool that helps law enforcement officials determine behavior. Using information about a person, such as his or her job, mental health, personal information, financial situation, and religious beliefs, can often give the negotiator some clues as to how the hostage-taker might respond to certain situations. If information reveals that the hostage-taker is a depressed or

Police officers in Alameda, California, carry a student during a hostage training exercise. Many law enforcement agencies hold regular training drills to increase their skills and preparation in the event that an incident occurs.

suicidal person, a negotiator will handle that person in a much different way than if information suggested that the person was a cold, rational criminal.

Negotiators begin by trying to create a sense of calm amid the tension. Negotiators will speak in a reassuring voice to hostage-takers and, at first, they will do more listening than talking in order to continue gathering information and earn the captors' trust. It is important that negotiators listen without judgment to the hostage-takers to create a sense of sympathy and humanity. This begins to establish a relationship between the negotiator and the hostage-taker.

Next, negotiators try to establish themselves as authority figures who can help the hostage-takers get food and medical care to the captors and captives alike. Once a sense of trust is established, a negotiator can begin to take small steps to move the situation along. If hostages are injured, a negotiator may want to speed up the pace of conversation and work to resolve the situation quickly. If the hostage-taker is demanding something, then a negotiator may try to delay things. All the while, the negotiator is managing the stress and tension of the situation. When this point is reached, monitoring the stress of the hostage-taker is important in order to wear him or her down without provoking an eruption of violence or desperation.

Conversations will eventually reveal what needs to be done to resolve the situation. Sometimes just talking to the hostage-takers is enough to get them to release hostages and give themselves up for arrest. The safe release of hostages is always the goal. If that doesn't work, then sometimes negotiators will ask for a "good faith" gesture. This might include releasing any children, older people, or hostages with medical problems first. Sometimes hostages are exchanged for concessions, which means something is given to the hostage-takers in exchange for the release of hostages.

However, sometimes there is no safe return of hostages or no way out for the hostage-takers, and the safety of the hostages becomes highly precarious. Negotiators must identify the point at which further negotiation is fruitless. At that point, communication with hostage-takers ceases, and law enforcement takes over.

CHAPTER THREE

GETTING STARTED IN THE FIELD

Becoming a crisis manager or hostage negotiator takes experience. These aren't positions that are filled by recent college graduates. Instead, they are coveted jobs that require years of experience and specialized training.

The foundation of a career in the field of crisis management and hostage negotiation is several years of working as a law enforcement officer or serving in the military. Experience in both law enforcement and the military exposes professionals to crisis situations on a regular basis. While preparation for each career path may vary, both crisis management and hostage negotiation require at least a bachelor's degree and a strong set of skills. These include:

- Strong communication skills
- Ability to handle high-stress situations
- Good decision-making skills

- Strong understanding of psychology and psychological conditions, such as depression and suicidal tendencies
- Strong understanding of the justice system
- Being comfortable in difficult situations
- Ability to be fair and open-minded
- Ability to handle people in varying types of situations
- Strong sense of responsibility and/or respect for authority
- Strong communication skills
- Excellent observation skills
- Good memory for details
- Being multilingual (as needed by region)

In addition, those interested in careers in law enforcement must fulfill additional requirements, such as:

- Passing background checks
- Possessing physical strength

Becoming a crisis manager or hostage negotiator takes years of training and requires a calm, confident demeanor. Many of these professionals begin their career in the military or as police officers. This is where they begin to gain experience in high-stress, high-stakes environments that test their resolve, maturity, and leadership abilities.

- Passing medical and vision exams
- Completing police academy training
- Completing additional training courses

Preparing for College

Students who are interested in careers in law enforcement should consider taking high school or community college courses in criminal justice and psychology. Criminal justice courses will introduce you to the basics of law enforcement and how the criminal justice system works. Psychology courses will offer an introduction to human behavior, which is important for understanding how and why criminals behave as they do. Both of these subjects will help prepare you for college and determine your aptitude and interest in law enforcement careers.

Students may also be interested in participating in explorer programs. These programs are designed for middle school and high school students who have an interest in pursuing a career in law enforcement. Explorer programs provide an overview of the different kinds of careers in law enforcement. Through hands-on activities, students engage in community service, simulate police training, and participate in ride-alongs.

For students interested in pursuing careers in crisis management and hostage negotiation, opportunities to shadow law enforcement officers will help shed light on the day-to-day duties of a police officer and the operations of a police department. Fairfax County (Virginia) police cadet Andre Marshall learns on the job by taking fingerprints.

High school graduates and college students can participate in the police cadets program. This law enforcement
apprenticeship program is for eighteen- to twenty-one-year-
olds and gives them the opportunity to experience the real
work that a police officer does. Cadets are paid and work
full-time or part-time for local police departments. Many
cadets use this experience to prepare themselves for the
rigors of the police academy.

College students interested in law enforcement careers
may want to learn more about their college's ROTC program.
ROTC, short for Reserve Officer Training Corps, is a training
program for students who wish to be commissioned officers
in the armed forces. Students receive military basic training
and leadership training. ROTC programs offer advanced
training in airborne school, mountain warfare school, air
assault school, and troop leadership training.

ROTC cadets are commissioned into the armed services
branch that most closely correlates to their training. There
are ROTC programs for the U.S. Army, Air Force, Marines,
Navy, and Coast Guard.

Choosing a Major

Many law enforcement professionals choose to major in
programs that give them direct knowledge of law enforcement, crime fighting, and security. These are all areas that
will help prepare a professional for day-to-day work in law
enforcement.

Criminal Justice

Criminal justice is the study of the justice system and the impact that social issues have on maintaining a fair and balanced society. This major examines the social and legal sides of criminal justice, from forensics and psychology to crime prevention and terrorism. Courses might include topics such as the court system, corrections, juvenile or youth justice, criminal law, crime and criminality, investigative techniques, evidence, and law enforcement in society.

Psychology

Psychology is the study of human behavior. This major helps build analytic skills and encourages critical thinking, both of which are crucial for law enforcement investigators who must review evidence of a crime and determine how the crime may have happened. Psychology majors also learn to collect, analyze, and interpret data. Courses in this major might include social psychology, abnormal psychology, perception, and behavior.

Law Enforcement Administration

Law enforcement administration is a program that educates students on how to manage and direct law enforcement agencies. It includes courses that help you learn to maintain social order, protect individual rights, and uphold the laws and

Police recruits complete courses and are trained in firearms, tactics, police science, law, and social science at a police academy. A background as a police officer can become the foundation for a career as a crisis manager or hostage negotiator.

institutions of democracy. Courses in leadership, organizational structures, and ethics help you become a responsible leader.

Homeland Security and Emergency Management

Homeland security and emergency management is a program that provides students with a broad view of homeland security issues, including policy, preparation, response, and recovery issues. Coursework covers law enforcement, emergency management, and business continuity.

Industrial and Labor Relations

Industrial and labor relations is a major that prepares students for

MAKE THE MOST OF YOUR INTERNSHIP

1. **Take the initiative.** Ask for opportunities to perform certain tasks or volunteer when a task needs to be assigned to someone.
2. **Meet as many people as possible.** Mingle with staff in other departments and ask what they do and how they got started in their careers. Shadow employees whose job is related to the one you are interested in. You might find out about a job you never knew existed, or you may get an inside look at how your industry really works.
3. **Attend professional events.** If your internship offers networking opportunities or educational seminars, take advantage of them. The whole reason you are doing an internship is to broaden your view of an industry and gain experience.
4. **Work on a variety of projects.** This gives you a lot of different types of work experience, which will be valuable once you start applying for full-time employment in your career field.
5. **Ask for feedback on your performance.** Take the time to ask how you are doing. Constructive feedback can help you learn from your mistakes.

6. **Ask questions. This is the opportunity to learn as much as you can about a career field or industry. Ask your supervisor or coworkers about their educational backgrounds, if they would do anything differently, how the job has changed since they started, how the company works, or how promotions and raises are awarded. This is the time for you to learn not only about your career field but also about the industry as a whole.**

leadership positions in business, law, government, international affairs, public policy, unions, and labor relations. Course work includes classes in government, history, law, economics, psychology, and sociology.

While a master's degree isn't required in the field of crisis management and hostage negotiation, further study could provide you with more specialized skills in a particular area of law enforcement, such as security, crime scene investigation, and criminal justice systems.

Internships: Experience Beyond the Classroom

Internships in law enforcement help students begin to gain professional, hands-on experience and may help with obtaining a first job. An internship is on-the-job training. Interns are usually college students looking to gain experience in a career field before they graduate. Interns can also be high school students interested in learning more about a career field before choosing a major in college.

Internships are the single most important way to gain experience in a career field. It is well documented that college students with internship experience on their résumés get more job offers and better salaries than those with no experience. Internships expose students to the day-to-day workings of a career field, offer entry-level training, allow students to apply the knowledge they have gained in the classroom to a real-world setting, help them narrow their career objectives, and give them valuable connections to professionals in the field.

The length of an internship can vary depending on the law enforcement agency offering the program. But usually internships are short-term assignments lasting a few weeks to a few months. Interns are assigned to a supervisor who oversees them and their work experience. The supervisor assigns tasks, assists in training the interns, and evaluates their performance. In both high school and college, internships can be completed for credit. In this case, a supervisor ensures that the required learning objectives are taking place and submits the proper forms necessary for the students to earn credit for their work.

For both the employer and the intern, the benefits of an internship are extensive. Employers are willing to hire interns with little or no experience. Interns provide extra staff at no additional cost, allowing a law enforcement agency to take on

Interning at a police station can give you insight into how law enforcement agencies function and their role in society. Ciara Cano *(left)* meets with Albuquerque (New Mexico) police officer Amanda Tapia on the final day of her internship with the police department.

more projects or accomplish tasks it could not otherwise complete without a larger staff and budget. For interns, working in the law enforcement field teaches valuable lessons that can only be learned on the job.

Whether paid on unpaid, the benefits of doing an internship reach far beyond a paycheck:

- **Gaining valuable work experience.**
  Coursework in a major related to law enforcement

or crisis management will teach the skills and theories of the field. But it's on-the-job training that gives students the opportunity to apply those skills. An internship provides the hands-on work experience that a student can't get in a classroom. For example, the Federal Bureau of Investigation (FBI) Volunteer Internship Program fosters learning in the various investigative techniques of the FBI. Interns work alongside professionals in areas such as counterterrorism, counterintelligence, field intelligence, cyber crime, white-collar crime, and civil rights. Gaining hands-on experience helps boost your résumé and makes you a strong candidate for future employment.

- **Giving yourself an edge in the job market.** Employers look at more than just your schoolwork or college major when they review your résumé. They want to see that you are interested in learning and that you will take the initiative. On-the-job experience shows them that you are already familiar with the law enforcement field, you have some entry-level skills, and you can hit the ground running if hired. Many employers prefer applicants who have done an internship or have relevant work experience. In many of the more competitive job markets, it is essential to set yourself apart from hundreds or even thousands of others competing for the same job.

- **Boosting your résumé.** Listing an internship experience boosts your résumé and makes you more attractive to employers. In a competitive job market, where there are hundreds or even thousands of applicants for every available job, every piece of experience that sets you apart is crucial and valuable.
- **Proving your skills.** You're not the only one who benefits from your internship. Employers view interns as prospective employees. Many law enforcement agencies use their internship programs as a way to scout talent for future jobs.
- **Deciding on the right career path.** An internship is great experience if you know what you want to do for a career. But, believe it or not, internships are also the best way to know if a career is wrong for you. Television crime dramas that show police officers chasing down criminals don't provide the best and most accurate examples of what law enforcement officers do on a daily basis. Many law enforcement jobs require long hours of desk work analyzing data and completing endless paperwork. The only way to learn what a career is really like day-in and day-out is to intern. Since internships are short-term, you can experience a career field without fully committing to it. Internships give you the chance to learn if this kind of work is or is not the right fit for you.

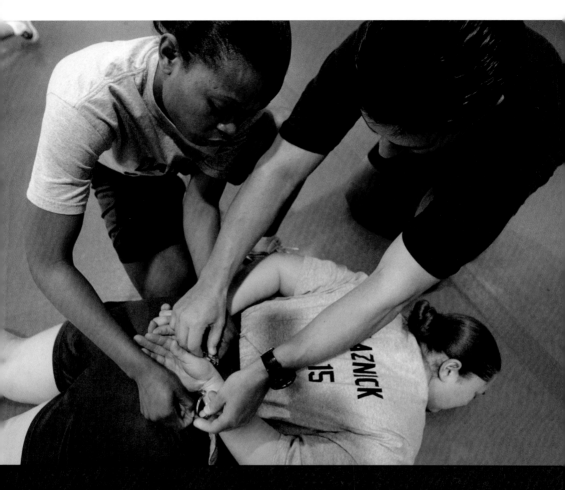

Recruits at the New York City Police Academy practice handcuffing techniques during a training exercise.

- **Applying classroom knowledge.** Classroom learning is essential to understanding concepts and theories, but without professional working experience that allows you to apply what you've learned, you're only getting half of the education you need.

An internship gives you the chance to apply the skills you learn in the classroom to real-world problems and situations.

- **Gaining confidence and maturity.**
  Experience builds confidence. An internship will give you a chance to gain experience that you can talk about on job interviews later. You'll also feel more confident when applying for jobs, knowing that your internships will make you a more marketable and impressive candidate than other job-seekers with little to no relevant experience. As a bonus, when you are interviewing for a job and you are asked if you know how to do a particular task, you can answer positively and recall what you learned on your internship.

CHAPTER FOUR

GETTING A JOB IN CRISIS MANAGEMENT OR HOSTAGE NEGOTIATION

The law enforcement field is booming. Between the advanced technology and weaponry now available to criminals and the focus on homeland security since the September 11 terrorist attacks and the 2013 Boston Marathon bombings, the demand for law enforcement professionals trained to meet the rigorous challenges facing our local and national security is on the rise.

Those who are trained in crisis management are able to anticipate and react to threats made to their organization, their workforce, their reputation, the safety of their employees, or the security of their country and its citizens. The Tylenol crisis outlined what can happen to a company and to public confidence when a product is tampered with and how crisis management can help lessen the impact of the problem for both the public and the company.

Launching your career in one of these exciting fields begins with getting a college degree and gaining experience in the field. Positions in hostage negotiation require prior work experience as a police officer or federal agent with an

Crisis managers handle more than just high-stakes events like bombing and hostage situations. They also help manage protests, like this rally organized by Occupy Wall Street, where law enforcement *(shown here)* push back protesters.

organization like the FBI. Jobs in crisis management can begin with a degree in programs such as communications, management, crisis communications, emergency management, or disaster management.

While you'll need to earn a college degree, there are things you can do to gain experience beyond your college coursework that will help you become an attractive candidate for a job. The first thing you'll want to do is look for an internship opportunity.

A police department intern participates in a simulated exercise with the local police department that involves an irate man. These types of exercises enable officers to train for a variety of scenarios.

Scoring an Opportunity

Obtaining an internship will take some work, but it will be time well spent. An internship is a great way to test out a career, learn about the day-to-day functions of a job, and see if the career is the right fit for you.

For careers in hostage negotiation, you'll want to identify internship opportunities with local, state, or federal law enforcement agencies. It is best to visit these organizations' Web sites to see what internships are available, when you can apply, and what the criteria are. At minimum, you'll need to have a high school diploma.

For careers in crisis management, you'll want to focus on finding internships

EXPLORING CAREERS

Exploring a career in crisis management and law enforcement can be an exciting thing to do. The types of jobs in both fields are wide ranging. Your first job in the field will begin to give you the experience that you need working with different types of people and in challenging situations that will help you hone your skills in crisis management and negotiation.

Career exploration activities give you a chance to learn about the different kinds of jobs in the crisis and law enforcement fields. But you will also get a chance to learn about yourself, your likes and dislikes, the types of jobs that best fit your personality, and where your true interests and skills lie. Self-assessment and aptitude tests are often the first type of activity a career counselor will engage you in to determine what your strengths are and identify your interests.

Another important first step is to familiarize yourself with job descriptions. You have decided that you want to be a crisis manager or hostage negotiator. But what do those jobs entail? By looking at job descriptions, you will begin to understand what qualifications you need (education, training, certifications, etc.) and what types of tasks you will perform on a day-to-day basis.

You should also learn what education and training are needed to enter the field. Like any career, you'll need an education and experience before you get started. For careers in the law enforcement field, that will include attending a police academy. Police academies offer courses in basic police training, police proficiencies and procedures, policing the local communities, and other subject areas related to law enforcement. For careers in crisis management, academic programs in management, emergency management, and communications can help give you a foundation to build on.

with organizations that deal with varying types of crises. You can find these positions within law enforcement and with private security firms and crisis management companies. These positions will help you gain experience in emergency response, rapid response, crisis management, reputation management, and strategic communications.

If you're a college student, your university's career services office can help you find your first internship or job. If you're in high school, you should start by making a list of law enforcement agencies in your geographical area. You could also learn more about internship opportunities by seeking an informational interview with a representative of a public agency or private company that interests you.

An informational interview helps you learn about an occupation from someone who has firsthand knowledge. You set up a time to talk to someone who has the career you'd like to work toward. Informational interviews are a chance to ask questions about how that person got started, what his or her educational background is, if he or she completed any additional or specific types of training, if he or she has any certifications, and what his or her day-to-day responsibilities are. You can also ask if there are other people you should talk to who have had different experiences. Not everyone found their way to a job in crisis management, law enforcement, and hostage negotiation by taking exactly the same path. Learning about others' career paths can help you understand that there are many different ways to arrive at your desired destination.

Most internships consist of learning about the organization, how it is staffed, its mission and activities, and any programs and services it offers. In many law enforcement internships, you may be assigned to a particular police unit or to a research project. At a crisis management internship, you'll often work with a crisis manager who will guide you throughout your internship. You'll contribute to projects, learn fundamental concepts of crisis and emergency management, and begin to build the skills that you need on the job.

Impress During the Interview

Job interviews are an opportunity for an employer to meet you in person, talk to you about your experience, and learn more about who you are. They are also a chance for you to learn more about the organization or agency you are interested in working for and gather more specific information about the day-to day activities of the job you applied for.

Most interviewers will begin by asking similar questions of each candidate to get to know them, followed by questions specific to your experience. How you answer each question helps a law enforcement agency understand who you are, what your personality is like, and how well you will work in high-pressure situations. Here are samples of questions that a law enforcement agency may ask you in an interview:

- **Tell me a little about yourself.** The interviewer is asking for a brief summary of your professional experience. Avoid giving overly specific and irrelevant details about your life story. What interviewers are looking for are facts about your education, specific law enforcement training you have completed, and your career aspirations.
- **Why are you interested in crisis management or law enforcement?** Interviewers want to know your motivation for pursuing a career in the field.

A job interview requires preparation and knowledge, especially for those seeking careers in law enforcement. Interviews in this career field are often more in depth, with candidates answering questions about their mental capacities, criminal record, motivation for pursuing a career in law enforcement, and ability to work in high-stress, high-pressure environments.

- **Do you have a police record?** It would be difficult for a candidate to hide his or her criminal history from a law enforcement agency. Your potential employer can and will easily find out if you have a record. In addition, most corporations and companies will also look into your background. Lying about it will be pointless and make the situation even worse. The best strategy is to never do anything that will earn you a police record in the first place.

- **Can you provide an example of a time when you remained calm during a tense and stressful event?** Interviewers are looking for your experience and your ability to stay cool, calm, and collected under pressure. Being in crisis management and law enforcement will put you in situations in which you'll need to rely on your patience, steadiness, and nerves of steel to achieve a successful resolution.

- **What are your strengths?** What this question is really asking is, why are you a great employee? Here's when you can boast about what you have to offer. If you thrive under pressure, are a great motivator, take initiative, are a good problem-solver, pay close attention to details, and are a hard worker, say so and provide real-life examples to back up your claims.

- **Are you a team player?** The answer to this question should always be yes. Crisis management and law enforcement are team-based professions. You will rely on your fellow officers and managers for information, support in stressful situations, and backup when a situation grows out of control. You need to be able to work together with people of all backgrounds. This might also be a good place to talk about leadership skills that you have developed.

The Hiring Process

The hiring process for careers in law enforcement is more involved than that for jobs in most other careers. Competition is strong and the application process is very thorough, often taking months to complete. While each law enforcement agency has its own hiring process, most will follow this pattern:

- **Initial application.** First, you should contact the law enforcement agency that you are interested in applying to and ask for or download an application. The application form allows the agency to prescreen applicants and obtain information such as your age, any prior criminal record, educational background, and employment history.
- **Written test.** The written test is an examination of your basic intellectual skills and abilities in areas such as reading comprehension, writing, direction following, judgment, reasoning, memory, and math. Based on the scores, candidates are ranked for further evaluation.
- **Personal history questionnaire and background check.** Investigators will look into

your records to verify information about your past and present life, including information about where you have lived, where you went to school, your employment history, your driving history, and your financial status.

- **Interview.** Interviews are a chance for you to talk about yourself in front of an individual or hiring committee, whose members want to hear more about you while interacting with you face-to-face. Questions will focus on everything from your personal history to information that investigators have discovered while conducting a

A career in law enforcement requires candidates to be physically fit. Police officers routinely have to subdue a suspect and engage in other physically challenging activities.

background check on you. These questions will test your mental stability, integrity, honesty, character, reputation in the community, and ability to think on your feet and react quickly to unexpected situations.

- **Physical test.** A physical test will find out how physically fit you are. At both the police academy and on the job, law enforcement officers face extreme physical demands that they must be ready for if they are to succeed.
- **Medical examination.** A complete medical exam, including drug testing, will give an agency an idea if there are any medical issues it should be aware of.
- **Psychological testing.** Law enforcement work can be psychologically stressful, and anyone not up to the mental and emotional rigors of the job needs to be weeded out. Anyone not up to the task can jeopardize the lives of his or her fellow officers and members of the public. The psychological test usually has two parts: a written portion and an interview with a psychologist.
- **Polygraph exam.** Not every agency administers a polygraph ("lie detector") test, but many do. A polygraph is used to make sure that you are telling the truth about your background and personal history.

CHAPTER FIVE

CAREER PATHS, SPECIALIZATIONS, AND JOB OUTLOOK

Careers in crisis management and hostage negotiation are exciting, dynamic positions. You will be on the front lines of a crisis where your decisions could directly affect the outcome and make the difference between success and failure, life and death. These are not careers for the faint of heart. These professions require strong conviction, courage, and absolute confidence.

With so many career paths to choose from—from FBI agent and police officer to hostage negotiator and crisis manager—choosing the path that meets your specific interests, aspirations, and aptitudes will take some research. All of these careers offer rewarding experiences. Overall, the job outlook for positions in crisis management and hostage negotiation is on the rise. Salaries vary depending on experience, educational requirements, and geographical location.

All of the following professions have common skills sets, though many have very specific educational requirements. They all require crisis management and hostage negotiation skills.

FBI Agent

Overview of job: FBI agents are in charge of investigating violations of national security and federal law. They might investigate kidnappings, bank robberies, terrorist acts, corruption, cyber crime, organized crime, and drug trafficking.

Typical tasks and skills: There is no typical day for FBI agents; their duties depend on whom or what they are investigating. In general, they observe suspects' activities, conduct research and background checks, interview persons of interest or witnesses, and occasionally go undercover to infiltrate a criminal group or organized crime ring. FBI agents should possess skills in multitasking, communication, good judgment, leadership, perceptiveness, and physical strength.

FBI agents routinely investigate kidnappings, bank robberies, terrorist acts, corruption, cyber crime, organized crime, and drug trafficking. Here, FBI agents are investigating the shootings at the Sandy Hook Elementary School in Newtown, Connecticut.

Requirements and special training: Those interested must be at least twenty-three years old (but younger than thirty-seven) to apply for a job as an FBI agent. At minimum, the applicant should be a graduate of a police academy. Most police academies now require applicants to have a college degree already. Applicants must pass an agent fitness exam. Once accepted into the FBI, they complete a twenty-week intensive training program at the FBI Academy in Quantico, Virginia, to prepare them for duty. Once training is completed, agents are assigned to field offices.

Professional credentials and certifications: After three years of work experience, an agent can apply to become an FBI Special Agent. Agents can also apply to become part of the Hostage Rescue Team, a counterterrorist group that specializes in hostage crisis situations. Additional special training courses are also available.

Future outlook: The U.S. Bureau of Labor Statistics (BLS) reports that the FBI is experiencing a record number of applicants. Jobs in the field are expected to grow as the U.S. government continues to support homeland security and counterterrorism activities.

Hostage Negotiator

Overview of job: Hostage negotiators are law enforcement officials trained to handle crisis situations that center on a person or group of people who have been taken hostage. Negotiators lead the hostage-takers to a peaceful resolution through psychological profiling, empathetic communication, persuasion, and reasoning. Hostage negotiators are predominantly employed by large police departments, such as the NYPD, and government agencies like the FBI.

Typical tasks and skills: While each crisis situation is different and hostage negotiators never have the same day on the job, there are many common skills that these professionals will use in most cases. They include establishing contact with the hostage-taker, communicating effectively with mentally unstable individuals, determining if there is room for negotiation, asking problem-solving questions to understand what the hostage-taker really wants, calming the hostage-taker and reducing his or her violent speech and threats, giving the hostage-taker something in order to get something larger in return, and getting the hostage-taker to like and trust the negotiator and view him or her in a favorable light.

Requirements and special training: Hostage negotiators have previous experience as police officers or federal agents. Special training provides the skills that they need to become a hostage negotiator. Training can differ between police departments and government agencies.

Professional credentials and certifications:
The FBI has a Hostage Rescue Team comprised of highly skilled individuals who have undergone extensive and intensive advanced training in psychology, negotiations, firearms, and counterterrorism. The National Council of Negotiation Associations provides additional training and courses that are available to officers interested in building and enhancing the skills they need to pursue careers in hostage negotiation. These programs focus on basic crisis negotiation, abnormal psychology, and understanding personality disorders.

Future outlook: The need for hostage negotiators is expected to grow as the federal government places increasing emphasis on homeland security and counterterrorism.

Police Officer

Overview of job: Police officers enforce laws, catch criminals, collect evidence, and patrol the community to prevent crime.

Typical tasks and skills: No day is typical for police officers. However, most work forty hours a week. Because police work is a twenty-four-hour-a-day job, officers can work day, evening, or overnight shifts. This is not a typical nine-to-five job. Many officers work longer hours, especially if they are working a case.

Metropolitan Transit Authority (MTA) officers in New York City screen packages and bags inside Grand Central Terminal, one of the city's two large train stations. MTA officers are responsible for the safety of the city's transit system.

Requirements and special training: Police officers must be U.S. citizens and must possess strong communication, logic, and perception skills. Applicants will undergo an extensive background check, written test, physical stamina test, personal interview, and polygraph test. Most law enforcement agencies and police departments prefer to hire applicants who have education at the associate's degree level or above, usually in criminal justice or law enforcement.

Professional credentials and certifications: Once they gain a minimum amount of experience, police officers can advance in their careers by taking additional training courses. These courses allow officers to learn the skills needed to become detectives and/or join special operations teams or units. These include the SWAT (Special Weapons and Tactics) team, street and gang units, internal affairs, hostage negotiation, or sex crimes units.

Future outlook: Employment for police officers is expected to increase over the next ten years. Nine out of ten police officers work for their local police departments, while the rest work at the state or federal levels. Candidates with college degrees in criminal justice and psychology or those with previous military experience will be the strongest candidates for future jobs.

Crisis Intervention Specialist/ Crisis Counselor

Overview of job: Crisis intervention specialists and crisis counselors advise, counsel, and provide treatment and therapy for people who have a variety of mental health and behavioral issues. They evaluate a person's mental health or behavior, develop treatment plans, set treatment goals, help people develop coping skills to modify and moderate behavior, and develop outreach programs to help others learn about and avoid destructive behavior. These specialists often work in the mental health field, but some are employed by law enforcement agencies and assist in crisis situations.

Typical tasks and skills: Crisis intervention specialists and crisis counselors spend most of their time meeting with people who need help learning how to control their behavior. They provide treatment, which can include counseling, and they coordinate care for their patients.

Requirements and special training: See "Professional credentials and certifications."

Professional credentials and certifications: Crisis intervention specialists and crisis counselors who work in private practice must be licensed. This requires a master's degree and two thousand to three thousand hours of supervised clinical experience. They must also pass state-recognized exams and continue their education with annual coursework. Specialists who work for law enforcement agencies or in other settings may be required to complete on-the-job training. Each state has its own specific and unique requirements.

Future outlook: Employment for crisis intervention specialists is expected to rise faster than the average for all occupations. Growth is due to more and more people turning to counselors to address personal issues or to complete treatment in lieu of jail time if their behavior is found to have been a factor in a crime.

Superstorm Sandy flooded homes and subway stations and forced the evacuation of thousands of residents in New York, New Jersey, and the surrounding areas. In the storm's wake, officers were assigned to monitor and assist citizens in the areas hardest hit by the disaster.

Crisis/ Emergency Managers

Overview of job:
Before, during, and after an event has occurred, crisis and emergency managers plan and direct disaster response and crisis management activities. They provide disaster preparedness training, develop emergency/crisis plans, and facilitate communication between the affected area and its population and law enforcement and the wider public.

Typical tasks and skills: There is no typical day for these professionals, since each crisis situation can vary, from a natural disaster to

JOB OPPORTUNITIES AT FEDERAL LAW ENFORCEMENT AGENCIES

Well-qualified candidates interested in job opportunities at federal law enforcement agencies should research the following governmental employers. Highly selective and very competitive, these employers offer stimulating and rewarding career opportunities for graduates of law enforcement, criminal justice, and other law-related academic programs.

- Bureau of Alcohol, Tobacco, Firearms, and Explosives (ATF)—The agency charged with investigating and preventing federal offenses involving the illegal use, manufacture, and possession of firearms; acts of arson and bombings; and illegal trafficking of alcohol and tobacco products.
- Bureau of Prisons—The agency responsible for the administration of the federal prison system.
- Central Intelligence Agency (CIA)—An intelligence-gathering agency that provides national security assessment.
- CIA National Clandestine Service—A division within the CIA with national authority for the

coordination, de-confliction (avoiding conflict among law enforcement agencies), and evaluation of clandestine (secret) operations across the intelligence community of the United States.

- **Department of Justice (DOJ)**—The agency responsible for the enforcement of the law and the administration of justice.
- **Drug Enforcement Administration (DEA)**—The agency that combats drug smuggling and use within the United States.
- **Federal Bureau of Investigation (FBI)**—The agency responsible for federal criminal investigations.
- **Federal Law Enforcement Training Center**— An interagency training center that serves to train officers from other federal law enforcement agencies.
- **INTERPOL**—Short for International Criminal Police Organization, the agency is an intergovernmental organization that encourages international law enforcement cooperation.
- **U.S. Secret Service**—An agency that provides protection to presidents and other high-level government officials and investigates financial crimes such as counterfeiting.

a hostage situation. In general, these professionals must have good communication skills, be able to keep calm under pressure, be able to think critically and make important decisions under pressure, and possess complex problem-solving skills. A solid knowledge of law enforcement, public safety, security, public relations, and leadership skills are necessary.

Requirements and special training: Crisis managers often have backgrounds in communication, emergency management, or administration. There are training courses that these professionals can complete to gain knowledge in specific areas of crisis management, such as hazard mitigation and preparedness, disaster response and recovery, and introduction to emergency management.

Professional credentials and certifications: Professionals can complete coursework leading to a Certified Emergency Manager designation, which is awarded by the International Association of Emergency Managers. The certification recognizes that professionals have the knowledge, skills, and ability to effectively lead and oversee an emergency management program.

Future outlook: Crisis management jobs are expected to grow faster than the average employment rate in this field.

Homeland Security Officer

Overview of job: Because of natural disasters like Superstorm Sandy and the increased threat of terrorist attacks, careers in homeland security have grown since the Department of Homeland Security (DHS) was created in 2001, following the tragic events of 9/11. Jobs as homeland security officers can include such varying duties as emergency preparedness, disaster relief, information security, intelligence analysis, border patrol, customs, and law enforcement.

Typical tasks and skills: Homeland security officers need to have skills and knowledge in basic law, ethics, emergency planning and response, and management and leadership. Typical tasks include responding to crisis situations; assisting in planning and executing emergency responses to varying types of situations; identifying threats; securing borders, airports, seaports, and waterways; researching and developing the latest security technologies; responding to natural disasters or terrorists assaults; and analyzing intelligence reports. Homeland security officers must be intelligent, understand the newest technologies, have the ability to break down intelligence, and be able to quickly inform the proper authorities if they detect any impending disasters.

Requirements and special training: Qualified applicants usually have a bachelor's degree in criminal justice or homeland security–related majors. Most professionals working in homeland security should be in good physical shape and understand the laws and regulations relating to their specialty.

Professional credentials and certifications:
Candidates will want to find degree programs that have been designated a National Center of Academic Excellence in Information Assurance Education by the National Security Agency (NSA) and the DHS. More than one hundred programs have this designation.

Future outlook: Jobs in this area are expected to grow with a number of employers, from federal agencies to private corporations, looking for the expertise that these positions bring. More DHS jobs are available, with job demand expected to increase. Homeland security is seeking experienced applicants, but there are still many positions available because of understaffing.

Public Relations Managers/Media Specialists

Overview of job: Public relations managers and specialists work to create and/or enhance the public image of an organization or public agency. These professionals build relations with the media, write and distribute press releases and news stories, create and carry out crisis communication plans, and provide information to the media about the organization or agency's mission and directives.

Typical tasks and skills: Public relations managers help prepare information for a number of audiences, from the local and national media to the employees of their organization or agency. They respond to requests for information, help employees of their organization or agency communicate effectively when being interviewed by the media, arrange interviews with the

Police officers are often the first source of communication for the public when an incident occurs. Here, Alabama state trooper Kevin Cook conducts a press conference in which he discusses the kidnapping of a five-year-old boy by Jimmy Lee Dykes, who was holding the child in an underground bunker on his property.

organization or agency's leadership, promote an organization or agency's programs and services, and work to strengthen the presence of the organization or agency in the community.

Requirements and special training: Public relations professionals need to obtain a college degree in communications, public relations, or English. They must be able to write well, speak clearly and effectively, and handle themselves professionally under pressure.

Professional credentials and certifications: The Public Relations Society of America offers a certification program for public relations professionals, though certification is not needed or required for employment.

Future outlook: Public relations is a growing field with numerous opportunities for advancement. The emergence of social media technologies and applications has helped create additional jobs in the field. Competition for entry-level jobs is strong, so candidates should seek opportunities, such as internships, to gain professional experience before graduating from college.

CHAPTER SIX

BUILDING A CAREER IN CRISIS MANAGEMENT AND HOSTAGE NEGOTIATION

O nce you've begun a career in law enforcement, communications, or crisis management, the next step in building your career is to complete additional training. This training will be in specialized topics related to crisis management and hostage negotiation.

Additional training opportunities might include coursework in advanced negotiation, understanding criminal behavior, negotiation theories, crisis communications, and applying psychology to tense situations. These advanced skills can be applied to your current position. You will be advancing your career with further study even as you are getting more on-the-job experience and hands-on skills. You will eventually become a sought-after expert in your field.

Once these advanced skills have been acquired, professionals are prepared to apply for positions as crisis managers and hostage negotiators. Most negotiators work on teams that are connected to special operations units, such as bomb squads, SWAT teams, or canine units. In more rural areas, negotiators

SWAT teams are special operations units comprised of the most qualified, highest-trained police officers. They respond to high-pressure, high-stakes situations that require specific types of training and skills.

may handle a dangerous situation only a few times a year. But for more urban areas, such as large cities like New York or Los Angeles, crisis managers and negotiators work regularly on cases and gain significant experience on the job.

Professional Qualifications, Certifications, and Licenses

Crisis managers and hostage negotiators must keep current with their skills. To accomplish this, they take professional

THE SHADOW KNOWS!

One of the best ways to gain experience is to "shadow" an experienced professional in crisis management or hostage negotiation. To shadow people at work is to stay close to them during their workday and observe everything that they do, asking questions, and listening to explanations about what, how, when, where, and why things are done in that particular job. Many law enforcement agencies and corporations have crisis managers or negotiators on staff, and they may be willing to have you shadow them.

These seasoned professionals can be invaluable assets to someone interested in learning about the job or gaining more experience. Experienced professionals can help you learn how a crisis or negotiation happens in real-world situations. While training sessions and courses will give you the skills you need, applying them in actual, real-world situations, where the outcome is much more unpredictable and the stakes far higher, can test your mettle and prove your abilities. Succeeding in real-life situations will help set you apart as you build your career.

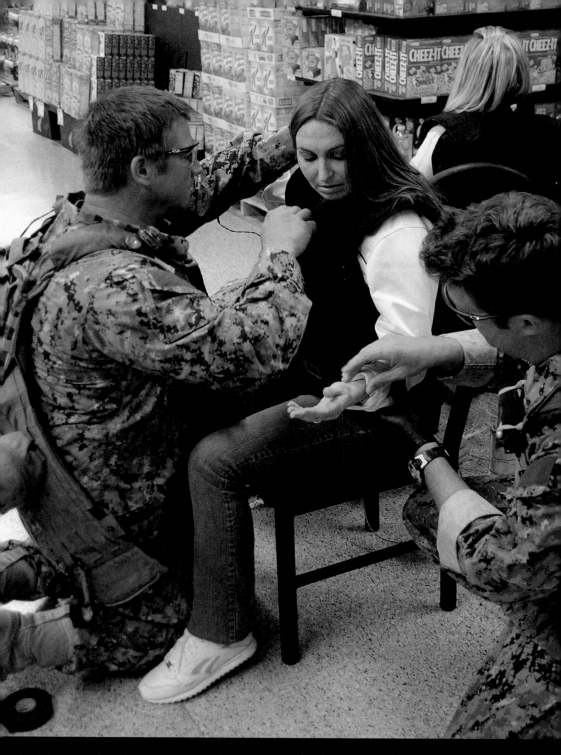

Intensive training exercises, like this one involving a hostage wearing a prop explosive device, are all part of the training that SWAT and special tactical teams undergo on a regular basis.

development courses that offer advanced knowledge in areas related to their fields. There are many different organizations that offer courses, seminars, and certifications. These allow professionals to build upon and expand their skills.

The Public Agency Training Council is the largest private law enforcement training organization. It offers more than one hundred courses in areas of interest to professionals in the law enforcement field. Some of its courses include Hostage Negotiations, Leadership Skills for Challenging Times, Tactical Communication Skills, and Crisis Communications for Dispatchers.

The Crisis Management Institute provides on-site crisis response, trauma intervention, and violence prevention on an as-needed basis, anywhere in the world. The organization also offers training and technical assistance in planning and developing crisis management plans. Its training courses are available on-site or online. They include Crisis Response Team Training, Organizational Structure and Pragmatics of Crisis Response, and Stellar Crisis Response Skill Building.

The Professional Crisis Management Association provides training, certification, and technology-based solutions to individuals and organizations. Its curriculum includes the courses Behavior Management and Crisis Prevention and Intervention. It also offers a Crisis Management Certification program. Other training includes the courses Crisis Management Practice Error Prevention and Management and Issues in Crisis Management.

The National Tactical Officers Association offers comprehensive conferences covering topics such as tactical operations training and crisis negotiations. In addition to full-scale conferences, the organization offers one-, three-, and five-day seminars such as Basic Crisis Negotiations, Negotiations for First Responders, and Advanced Crisis Negotiations.

The Institute for Law Enforcement Administration provides courses, seminars, and workshops for law enforcement agencies both nationally and internationally. These include Ethical Decision Making, Police-Media Relations, and Communicating in Crisis.

Special Operations Teams

In times of national and international security threats, special operations teams are called in to provide guidance and experience in crisis management and hostage negotiation. This is the purpose of the FBI's Hostage Rescue Team (HRT). The HRT was established in 1983 to be a national-level counterterrorism unit capable of responding to hostage situations both within the United States and around the world. The team i based in Quantico, Virginia, at the FBI headquarters.

The HRT is a highly trained group of law enforcemer officers who handle missions related to hostage negotia and rescue, high-risk raids, manhunt operations, mariti

The FBI's Hostage Rescue Team is a highly experienced and capable group of law enforcement officers trained to handle hostage negotiation and rescue, manhunts, raids, and maritime and extreme weather operations.

operations, extreme weather operations, and protection for dignitaries and FBI personnel overseas.

To become a member of the HRT, candidates must be fully qualified as Special Agents and possess special tactical qualifications. Once a candidate has two years of experience as a Special Agent, he or she can apply to compete for a place on the HRT team. This requires a two-week selection course where candidates will be tested on a variety of skills, including physical fitness, firearms skills, problem-solving ability, leadership, team compatibility, and other credentials. If accepted, HRT members are required to commit to a minimum of four years with the HRT.

Volunteer

Some law enforcement agencies have Police Reserve Officer programs. These programs are comprised of community members who volunteer their time at a local law enforcement agency. Reserve officers receive much of the same training as police officers, but these positions are voluntary and not paid. They are a great way for a person who wants to gain more experience in law enforcement to get a better understanding of how a police agency works and the responsibilities of a police officer.

Another way to get experience in law enforcement is to become part of a police auxiliary program. These volunteers perform roles similar to police reserve officers, but there are usually age requirements. Not every state in the country uses a police auxiliary, so those interested in these roles will have to research their geographical area for more information on available opportunities.

airborne Transported or carried by the air.

apprentice One who is learning, by practical experience and under skilled workers, a trade, art, or calling.

aptitude One's natural ability or capacity for learning.

bystander Someone who is present but not taking part in a situation or event.

civilian A person who is not on active duty in the armed services and not on a police or firefighting force; an ordinary citizen.

commissioned officer An officer who holds a commission and ranks as a second lieutenant or above in the U.S. Army, Navy, Air Force, or Marine Corps.

concession The act of conceding, or giving in or compromising, on something.

counterterrorism The practices, tactics, techniques, and strategies that governments, militaries, police departments, and corporations adopt to fight against terrorist threats and/or acts.

cyanide A type of poison.

democracy A government by and for the people, or a rule of the majority; a government in which the supreme power is vested in the people and exercised by them directly or indirectly through a system of representation usually involving periodically held free elections.

ethics A set of moral principles.

evidence Something that provides proof of something (for example, a crime committed in a certain way by a certain person).

extremist Someone who advocates extreme measures or views.

humanity The human race; the quality or state of being human; the quality or state of being humane, or compassionate and sympathetic.

labor relations The study and practice of managing unionized employment situations.

multilingual The ability to communicate in more than one language.

perception Observation; a mental image; awareness of the surrounding environment through physical sensation; a capacity for comprehension.

political uprising A series of demonstrations, amounting to a sustained campaign of civil resistance that is aimed at achieving regime change and/or greater political freedom and equality.

protocol A code prescribing strict adherence to correct etiquette or behavior.

psychological profile A behavioral and investigative tool intended to help investigators accurately predict and profile the characteristics, tendencies, and motivations of unknown criminal subjects or offenders.

warfare Military operations between enemies.

FOR MORE INFORMATION

Bureau of Alcohol, Tobacco, Firearms and Explosives (ATF)
Office of Public and Governmental Affairs
99 New York Avenue NE, Room 5S 144
Washington, DC 20226
(800) 800-3855
Web site: http://www.atf.gov
The ATF protects communities from violent criminals, criminal organizations, the illegal use and trafficking of firearms, the illegal use and storage of explosives, acts of arson and bombings, acts of terrorism, and the illegal diversion of alcohol and tobacco products. It partners with communities, industries, law enforcement, and public safety agencies to safeguard the public through information sharing, training, research, and technology.

Canadian Police College (CPC)
P.O. Box 8900
Ottawa, ON K1G 3J2
Canada
(613) 993-9500
Web site: http://www.cpc.gc.ca
The CPC provides advanced and specialized training and executive development to law enforcement officers from all jurisdictions to help them combat crime and increase Canadians' safety. Through its highly trained staff and subject-matter experts, the CPC offers a suite of over fifty-five advanced and specialized courses and workshops in investigative techniques, technological crime, forensic identification, explosives disposal/investigations, police executive development, and professional development.

Crisis Management Institute (CRI)
P.O. Box 331
Salem, OR 97308
(503) 585-3484
Web site: http://www.cmionline.com
The CRI provides services that include on-site crisis response, trauma intervention, and violence prevention at the time of need anywhere in the world. It also offers training and technical assistance in planning and development stages.

Federal Bureau of Investigation (FBI)
FBI Headquarters
935 Pennsylvania Avenue NW
Washington, DC 20535-0001
(202) 324-3000
Web site: http://www.fbi.gov
The FBI's mission is to protect and defend the United States against terrorist and foreign intelligence threats and to enforce the criminal laws of the United States.

Federal Emergency Management Agency (FEMA)
U.S. Department of Homeland Security
500 C Street SW
Washington, DC 20472
(202) 646-2500
Web site: http://www.fema.gov
FEMA's mission is to support citizens and first responders to ensure that as a nation we work together to build, sustain, and improve our capability to prepare for, protect against, respond to, recover from, and mitigate all hazards.

Institute for Law Enforcement Administration (ILEA)
5201 Democracy Drive

Plano, TX 75024-3561
(972) 244-3430
Web site: http://www.cailaw.org/ilea
The ILEA is an educational center designed to enhance the
professional development of police leaders at all levels.
Hundreds of police executives, managers, and supervi-
sors who have graduated from the institute serve in law
enforcement leadership positions around the world.
Membership in the ILEA is available to city, county, state,
and federal law enforcement organizations.

International Crisis Management Association (ICMA)
Sovereign Court
230 Upper 5th Street
Milton Keynes, England MK9 2HR
Web site: http://www.icma-web.org.uk
The International Crisis Management Association was established to respond to a growing need to develop and
exchange knowledge in the field of crisis management at
the international level, provide a forum for discussion and
research, and network and share information.

Marsh Canada Ltd.
161 Bay Street, Suite 1400
Toronto, ON M5J 2S4
Canada
(416) 868-2600
Web site: http://canada.marsh.com
Marsh Canada believes that the ability to manage a crisis
effectively is the result of an in-depth understanding of
risk, thorough crisis management planning, and a strategy for maintaining risk assessment and crisis reaction
capabilities. It offers companies the crisis management
structure, communications, and strategies necessary to

assess a situation quickly, deploy resources effectively, and execute an emergency response flawlessly.

National Tactical Officers Association (NTOA)
P.O. Box 797
Doylestown, PA 18901
(800) 279-9127
Web site: http://ntoa.org
The mission of the National Tactical Officers Association is to enhance the performance and professional status of law enforcement personnel by providing a credible and proven training resource, as well as a forum for the development of tactics and information exchange. Its ultimate goal is to improve public safety and domestic security through training, education, and tactical excellence.

Professional Crisis Management Association (PCMA)
10269 NW 46 Street
Sunrise, FL 33351
(954) 746-0165
Web site: http://www.pcma.com
The PCMA provides crisis management and behavior analysis training, certification, consulting, and technology-based solutions that help individuals and organizations.

Public Agency Training Council (PATC)
5235 Decatur Boulevard
Indianapolis, IN 46241
(800) 365-0119
Web site: http://www.patc.com
The PATC is the largest privately held law enforcement training company in the nation, offering a curriculum of over one

hundred topics of academy-quality training programs throughout the United States by open registration, in-service, and co-hosted programs. Its instructors bring years of hands-on experience in their areas of expertise and instructional fields.

U.S. Department of Homeland Security (DHS)
Washington, DC 20528
(202) 282-8000
Web site: http://www.dhs.gov
The mission of the Department of Homeland Security is to ensure a homeland that is safe, secure, and resilient against terrorism and other hazards.

Western States Hostage Negotiator's Association (WSHNA)
2416 46th Avenue SE
Puyallup, WA 98374-4181
(253) 446-6119
Web site: http://wshna.com
The goal of this association is to develop in its members a higher degree of proficiency in the performance of their professional duties. It provides training for members and acts as a resource and conduit for information sharing.

Web Sites

Due to the changing nature of Internet links, Rosen Publishing has developed an online list of Web sites related to the subject of this book. This site is updated regularly. Please use this link to access the list:

http://www.rosenlinks.com/LAW/Host

Brezina, Corona. *Careers in Law Enforcement* (Careers in Criminal Justice). New York, NY: Rosen Publishing, 2009.

Dempsey, John S., and Linda S. Forst. *An Introduction to Policing.* Independence, KY: Delmar Cengage Learning, 2013.

Fremont-Barnes, Gregory. *Rescue at the Iranian Embassy: The Most Daring SAS Raid* (The Most Daring Raids in History). New York, NY: Rosen Publishing, 2011.

Harmon, Daniel E. *Careers in the Corrections System.* New York, NY: Rosen Publishing, 2009.

Immell, Myra. *At Issue: Homeland Security.* Farmington Hills, MI: Greenhaven Press, 2009.

Learning Press Editors. *Becoming a Homeland Security Professional.* New York, NY: Learning Express, LLC, 2010.

McNab, Chris, and Howard Gerrard. *Storming Flight 181— GSG-9 and the Mogadishu Hijack 1977.* Oxford, England: Osprey Publishing, 2011.

Meyer, Jared. *Homeland Security Officer* (Extreme Careers). New York, NY: Rosen Publishing, 2007.

Misino, Dominick J. *Negotiate and Win: Unbeatable Real-World Strategies from the NYPD's Top Negotiator.* New York, NY: McGraw-Hill, 2004.

Mullins, Matt. *Homeland Security.* North Mankato, MN: Cherry Lake Publishing, 2010.

Noesner, Gary. *Stalling for Time: My Life as an FBI Hostage Negotiator.* New York, NY: Random House, 2010.

Sterngass, Jon. *Great Careers with a High School Diploma: Public Safety, Law, and Security.* New York, NY: Facts on File, 2008.

Streissguth, Tom. *The Security Agencies of the United States: How the CIA, FBI, NSA, and Homeland Security Keep Us Safe.* Berkeley Heights, NJ: Enslow Publishing, 2012.

Watson, Stephanie. *A Career as a Police Officer.* New York, NY: Rosen Publishing, 2010.

Woog, Adam. *Careers in the Secret Service.* New York, NY: Benchmark Books, 2012.

Woog, Adam. *Careers in State, County, and City Police Forces.* New York, NY: Benchmark Books, 2012.

Bernstein, Alan B., and Cindy Rakowitz. *Emergency Public Relations: Crisis Management in a 3.0 World.* Bloomington, IN: Xlibris, 2012.

ChangingMinds.org. "About Hostage Negotiations." Retrieved January 2013 (http://changingminds.org/disciplines/negotiation/styles/hostage_negotiations.htm).

ChangingMinds.org. "Hostage Negotiations." Retrieved January 2013 (http://changingminds.org/disciplines/negotiation/styles/hostage_negotiations.htm).

Coombs, W. Timothy. "Crisis Management and Communications." Institute for Public Relations, October 30, 2007. Retrieved January 2013 (http://www.instituteforpr.org/topics/crisis-management-and-communications).

Grabianowski, Ed. "How Hostage Negotiation Works." HowStuffWorks.com. Retrieved January 2013 (http://people.howstuffworks.com/hostage-negotiation.htm).

Hogan, David. "Follow These Rules for Better Crisis Management." ReporterNews.com, September 4, 2012. Retrieved January 2013 (http://www.reporternews.com/news/2012/sep/04/follow-these-rules-better-crisis-management).

Kemp, Joe. "40 Years Ago Today, John Wojtowicz Held Brooklyn Bank Hostage Inspiring Al Pacino Movie 'Dog Day Afternoon' and Giving Birth to NYPD unit." *New York Daily News*, August 21, 2012. Retrieved January 2013 (http://www.nydailynews.com/new-york/brooklyn/40-years-today-john-wojtowicz-held-brooklyn-bank-hostage-inspiring-al-pacino-movie-dog-day-afternoon-giving-birth-nypd-unit-article-1.1141608#ixzz2JHr5cdiP).

Lohr, David. "Remembering Attica Prison: The 'Bloodiest One-Day Encounter Between Americans Since the Civil War.'" *Huffington Post*, September 13, 2012. Retrieved January 2013 (http://www.huffingtonpost.com/2012/09/13/attica-prison_n_1880737.html).

Mack, Sonja. "6 Tips for Crisis Management." BlackEnterprise.com, October 19, 2010. Retrieved January 2013 (http://www.blackenterprise.com/small-business/6-tips-for-crisis-management).

McMains, Michael J., and Wayman C. Mullins. *Crisis Negotiations: Managing Critical Incidents and Hostage Situations in Law Enforcement and Corrections.* Los Angeles, CA: Anderson Publishing, 2010.

Military.com. "Tracking Down a Career in Law Enforcement." Retrieved January 2013 (http://www.military.com/veteran-jobs/search/law-enforcement-jobs/find-a-career-in-law-enforcement.html).

Misino, Dominick J., and Hugh McGowan. "Hostage Negotiator Certification: Necessary or Not?" Public Agency Training Council. Retrieved January 2013 (http://www.patc.com/weeklyarticles/host_negotiator.shtml).

New York Times. "Ask a Hostage Negotiator." September 10, 2012. Retrieved January 2013 (http://cityroom.blogs.nytimes.com/2012/09/10/ask-a-hostage-negotiator).

Phillips, Brenda D., David M. Neal, and Garry R. Webb. *Introduction to Emergency Management.* Boca Raton, FL: CRC Press, 2011.

Slatkin, Arthur A. *Communication in Crisis and Hostage Negotiations: Practical Communication Techniques, Stratagems, and Strategies for Law Enforcement, Corrections, and Emergency Service Personnel.* Springfield, IL: Charles C. Thomas Publishing, Ltd., 2010.

Slatkin, Arthur A. *Training Strategies for Crisis and Hostage Negotiations: Scenario Writing and Creative Variations for Role Play.* Springfield, IL: Charles C. Thomas Publishing, Ltd., 2009.

Time. "The Nation: The War at Attica: Was There No Other Way?" September 27, 1971. Retrieved January 2013 (http://www.time.com/time/magazine/article/0,9171,910027,00.html).

University of Florida Interactive Media Lab. "Effective Crisis Management: The Exxon Crisis, 1989." Retrieved January 25, 2013 (http://iml.jou.ufl.edu/projects/fall02/susi/exxon.htm).

University of Florida Interactive Media Lab. "Effective Crisis Management: The Tylenol Crisis, 1982." 2002. Retrieved January 2013 (http://iml.jou.ufl.edu/projects/fall02/susi/tylenol.htm).

About the Author

Laura La Bella is a writer and editor who has written numerous books on safety, security, emerging threats, and careers, including *World Financial Meltdown*; *Not Enough to Drink: Pollution, Drought, and Tainted Water Supplies*; *Safety and the Food Supply*; *Careers in Web Development*; *Dream Jobs in Sports Fitness and Medicine*; and *Internship and Volunteer Opportunities for People Who Love to Build Things*. La Bella lives in Rochester, New York, with her husband and son.

Photo Credits

Cover U.S. Air Force photo/Airman 1st Class Veronica Pierce; pp. (background image) 6–7 clearviewstock/Shutterstock.com; p. 7 Bruce R. Bennett/ZumaPress/Newscom; pp. 9, 24, 41, 58, 71, 89 iStockphoto/Thinkstock; p. 10 Santi Visalli/Archive Photos/Getty Images; pp. 12–13, 26–27, 29, 36–37, 69 © AP Images; pp. 17, 21 New York Daily News Archive/Getty Images; pp. 32–33 Baltimore Sun/McClatchy-Tribune/Getty Images; pp. 38–39 Justin Sullivan/Getty Images; pp. 42–43 U.S. Air Force photo/Staff Sgt. Jonathan Snyder; pp. 44–45 The Washington Times/Zuma Press/Newscom; pp. 48–49, 56, 77 Mario Tama/Getty Images; pp. 53, 60–61 © Marla Brose/Albuquerque Journal/ZUMA Press; p. 59 Andrew Burton/Getty Images; p. 66 Stephen Coburn/Shutterstock.com; pp. 72–73 Michael Bocchieri/Getty Images; pp. 80–81 Paul J. Richards/AFP/Getty Images; p. 87 AP Images/al.com/Joe Songer; p. 90 MILpictures by Tom Weber/The Image Bank/Getty Images; p. 92 U.S. Navy photo by MC Seaman Apprentice Damian Berg; pp. 94–95 FBI; cover and interior pages background textures Alex Gontar/Shutterstock.com, Eky Studio/Shutterstock.com, Andreas Liem/Shutterstock.com.

Designer: Michael Moy; Photo Researcher: Karen Huang